THE GUIDE TO HOSTING INTERNATIONAL STUDENTS IN CANADA

MONIKA FERENCZY

Horizon Educational Consulting/Conseillers en Education
www.horizoned.ca

The Guide to Hosting International Students in Canada
Copyright © 2020 by Monika Ferenczy

All rights reserved. No part of this publication may be reproduced, distributed, or transmitted in any form or by any means, including photocopying, recording, or other electronic or mechanical methods, without the prior written permission of the author, except in the case of brief quotations embodied in critical reviews and certain other non-commercial uses permitted by copyright law.

Tellwell Talent
www.tellwell.ca

ISBN
978-0-2288-2186-1 (Paperback)
978-0-2288-2185-4 (eBook)

TABLE OF CONTENTS

Acknowledgments v

1 Introduction 1
2 When students arrive in Canada for the first time 3
3 What to explain first: the basics 9
    Food 9
    Internet connection 10
    Household routines 11
    Hygiene 13
    Clothing 14
    Weather 15
    Transportation 17
4 Adapting to Life in Canada 19
    Appliance use: bathroom, laundry, kitchen 19
    Heating, water use and hydro 25
    Family structures and inclusion 30
    Communication: Verbal and non verbal
        communication (body language) 31
    Extracurricular activities and sports, fitness 35
    Customs: a bit of 'Canadiana' and
        transitioning to living like a local 37
5 Health and Personal Safety 44
    Physical health 44
    Mental health 46
6 Conclusion 53

Appendix 1: Sample instructions for students 55
Appendix 2: Posting Rules and expectations 57
About the Author 63

ACKNOWLEDGMENTS

Many thanks to the individuals who host students and guide them into adjusting to life in Canada and those involved with assisting international students as hosts, teachers and agents
and to many others for their valuable input and feedback.
Special thanks to Claudette Andress, Jennifer Olchowy and Johanna Ziegler
for proofreading and editing
and Pierre Carriere for his enduring support

Introduction

Canada has welcomed many individuals and families since becoming a sovereign nation in 1867, whether immigrants or refugees. A new demographic influx has exponentially increased in the last five years which is due to global mobility and access to educational opportunities for foreigners in Canada.

International students make up a much larger part of the student population at post-secondary institutions, more so at colleges than universities. This trend also continues to grow in the high school sector, with school boards engaging in student recruitment from all parts of the world. The additional funding that international students bring through tuition fees has been a new source of revenue for these institutions, and many colleges and universities now actively recruit students at oversees education fairs.

In response to the rising number of students arriving to study in Canada, related services such as housing and educational support services to help in transitioning these students has proportionately increased in every major city in Canada.

Accommodations include student residence spaces on campus, off campus condominium purchases and rentals,

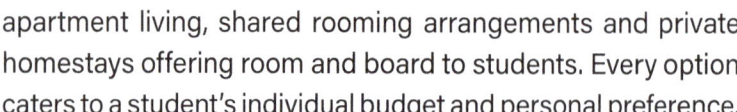

apartment living, shared rooming arrangements and private homestays offering room and board to students. Every option caters to a student's individual budget and personal preference.

All students must show financial security prior to being granted a study permit to come to Canada, regardless of the age of the student. Mature students often arrive with their spouses and young children. Young adults and adolescents tend to arrive alone, being the first of their families to venture out on an international education pathway.

It is important that students feel welcomed in Canada from the moment of their arrival until their needs have been met. Acclimatization to living in Canada may take up to two years. We wish for them to thrive and not just survive, as many will stay on and become permanent residents and seek employment in our communities, furthering economic growth for our nation.

This guide will help all those who work with international students and, or, host them, to facilitate a smooth transition to life in Canada so that they may enjoy their educational experience. This initiative will ensure that their first impressions of Canada are positive, and our great nation's image is preserved for the current and next generation of newcomers.

When students arrive in Canada for the first time

Arriving to a new country can be a daunting experience, particularly if the individual's language skills are not yet proficient in either official language. Depending on their point of entry, it can be a large cosmopolitan centre like Toronto, Vancouver or Montreal or smaller cities and towns across Canada, from the Maritimes to across the Prairies.

AIRPORT PICKUP

It is important to offer international students pick up at the airport, bus or train station when they arrive. This should be confirmed with the student prior to arrival by requesting travel itineraries and arrival dates and times. Greeting a student into a new country by the contact person is the first gesture of welcome and establishing a personal connection.

If another person from the original contact person is to provide pickup through the family, organization or institution, a picture of this individual should be sent to the student. The student should also forward a good quality recent photo in addition

to the photocopy of their passport picture page, in order to correctly identify the student at pickup. Most students will arrive by plane, unless their destination place of study is further away from an airport.

Indicate to the student where he or she will be picked up according to pre-arranged meeting point at the airport or bus or train terminal. This area is usually the baggage carrousel section as students will be arriving with one or several suitcases. The individual should be met personally inside the terminal and foreigners should not be expected to be familiar with drop off and pick up locations and practices at terminals. This means that parking fees should be anticipated for the student pick up day and time.

Traffic conditions should also be anticipated so that arrival can be timed to personally meet and greet the student and incorporate the time necessary for the student's flight

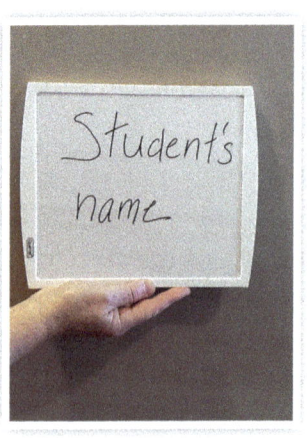

to land, disembark the plane, clear customs and pick up their baggage at the luggage carrousel. This process could take up to an hour after the flight has landed in busy airport centres.

Once at the airport, a personal sign on a small whiteboard or piece of cardboard with the student's name on it should be used to identify the greeter to the student. It should be prominently visible and held up at chest or eye level in the luggage carrousel area where the flight number is indicating corresponding baggage arrival from the student's flight.

The student may think that it is possible to call or text in the new country via cellphone but may not have engaged their roaming services or connected to the WIFI service in the airport to enable wireless communication. A sign ensures that a student will locate the contact person expecting him or her.

Nevertheless, provide your phone number so that the student or any official can contact you.

GREETING THE STUDENT AND CULTURAL SENSITIVITY

Once the student and pick up person have found one another, the student should be greeted with a smile and a welcoming statement such as *"Welcome to Canada! It's nice to meet you"* and introduce the name of the person greeting him or her *"My name is..."*.

Although a hand can be extended for a handshake, many students will have carry on luggage in their hands making this awkward. They also may not be familiar with this custom and may not be comfortable with personally touching another person they have not previously met. Eye contact may not always be present, as this has culturally different meaning in some foreign countries.

Keep conversation short, clear and functional and focused on their belongings such as

"What colour is your suitcase? How many bags do you have?"

but wait for the response to the first question before asking a second question. A tendency to gush in excitement at meeting the student for some individuals, can result in unintentional bombarding of too many questions and information overload for the weary traveller.

Making small talk with newcomers may be confusing to them and they may be tired and not able to converse fully in their second or additional language at the time of their arrival.

Ask the student if he or she needs to use a washroom before leaving the terminal, particularly if there is still a long drive ahead to reach the accommodation location.

Offering the student a bottle of water once inside the vehicle, is also welcoming, as water is a familiar object of sustenance in every country.

Indicate to the student how long it will take to reach their accommodation destination. Many students have little knowledge of Canada upon arriving and the concept of time and travel in terms of distance between places will be unfamiliar to them.

It is acceptable to ride in silence and not speak to the student as they may appreciate a few moments of quiet relaxation knowing that they are securely on the last leg of their journey with someone to guide them.

Some students may have been travelling for over 24 hours by the time they arrive in Canada and may not yet have travelled outside of their home country. Having someone drive them to their final destination is a great stress relief for first time travellers.

TAXI AND UBER

If it impossible for the student to be picked up upon arrival for various reasons, or they arrive late because of flight delays and pick up cannot be organized, provide taxi and Uber information prior to arrival so that a secondary plan can be put in place in case of unexpected events or delays.

Included in this information should be the approximate cost of the transfer from the airport to the accommodation destination and whether it can be paid in cash or by credit card. Some international credit cards do not work initially in Canada and it is advisable that students purchase some Canadian currency prior to arrival or at the airport upon arrival to pay for fares.

Bus transportation information is not advised as it will be too difficult to navigate for a newcomer and challenging to use with suitcases.

What to explain first: the basics

FOOD

Once the student arrives at the accommodation location ensure that there is more drinking water available and some food on hand to offer. Many travellers will be very hungry as access to food in transit is often challenging, or food brought with them for the journey has been thrown out by customs officials (this often happens with first time travellers who are not aware that unpackaged food such as meat and fruit will not be allowed in Canada upon arrival).

Depending on the season in which the student arrives, a hot beverage or food can be offered such as tea, soup, rice or noodle bowl or a full meal. If the student is not hungry, or in summer time, a cold beverage, fruit and snacks, can offered as lighter fare.

Especially for the first couple of nights, ensure that they have access to snacks and drinks as they might wake up during the night due to jetlag and become hungry.

Do not be offended if a student chooses not to eat, as he or she may be uncomfortable with unfamiliar food choices which differ from their base diets in the home country. Transitioning to local food and diet is often challenging, particularly for individuals from cultures that are far removed from the Canadian, North American or European context.

Explain to the student where food is available around the residence neighbourhood and when the next scheduled meal time will take place. Also indicate what they may help themselves to in the fridge, kitchen cupboards or pantry area. Be aware that some students may be unfamiliar with kitchen appliances.

INTERNET CONNECTION

Provide internet connectivity such as WIFI passwords to the student upon arrival as many students will want to notify family members back home that they have arrived safely to their new destination.

Helping the student to send a message to their family is always a kind gesture to ensure that her/his parents know that he/she has arrived safely.

Show them how to download translation apps on their cellphone to assist them if their language skills are still weak.

Explain and provide written notes on band width, upload and download speeds on the network, additional charges and restricted hours of use if they exist in the context of the residence.

Some of the apps that students use for world wide communication may vary based on their home country. For example, Facebook is banned in China and students use the WeChat or 'qq' platform to communicate. Others may use other platforms such as WhatsApp.

Help students with setting up a new phone while in Canada by providing information on local stores, phone plan providers and rates, or student deals.

Opening a bank account as soon as the student has a copy of his or her timetable (required as proof of enrollment by the banking institution) is also important to enable online banking features and debit and credit card payments. Student credit card plans are available for those whose international banking cards do not function in local stores in smaller communities. Often these cards have limited use and are only recognized by big store chains, hotels and tourist related venues.

HOUSEHOLD ROUTINES

Provide the student with a key or passcode to your main door entry so that he or she can come and go according to personal schedule.

Post a schedule of hours to the student if he or she is in a student residence, noise curfews and other rules if sharing a home or apartment accommodation. It is best to write out the rules that are to be expected and post these on the wall or provide a copy to the student for quick reference.

The Appendix provides a sample of the types of posted information that can be displayed in either the student's

room, a common area such as kitchen, lounge or laundry room, or provided in an orientation handbook.

Many students with weak language communication rely on printed text to scaffold their language learning skills. Written reminders, sticky notes or posted rules are very effective to explain expectations on a daily basis with international students.

THE GUIDE TO HOSTING INTERNATIONAL STUDENTS IN CANADA

HYGIENE

Students come from all parts of the world, each having different customs regarding personal hygiene, toilet use and bathing rituals.

Examples of toilets in Asia, Africa and the Middle East

It is important to explain to the student that in Canada, a daily shower is the norm, sometimes two a day in hot summer weather and that strong body odour is not well received in public, in school or work locations or in shared living accommodations.

Although Canadians are known to be polite citizens and will often not comment on another person's hygiene for risk of offense, this initiative should not be overlooked when an international student arrives and is unaware of societal customs.

If it is too delicate a subject to broach in person, a written explanation and some sample products can be left for the student in his or her room as part of a welcome package, or in the bathroom as part of complimentary toiletries upon arrival.

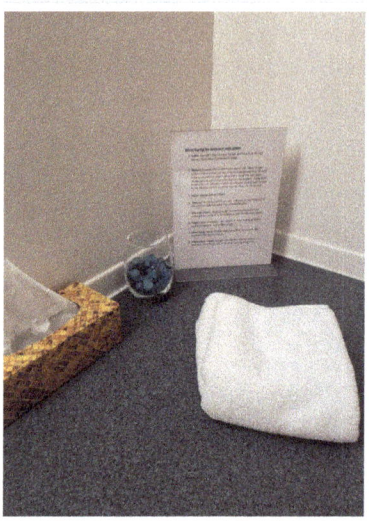

A sample cultural cue card can be found in the Appendix to help address this matter.

CLOTHING

If a student arrives in Canada in January or February for a mid-year start or academic study period, it is essential to have them show you what they brought in their suitcase and provide them with a list of critical wardrobe pieces. Many students from warm and hot countries will thought to have brought warm clothing with a couple of sweaters and a light jacket but the cold harshness of winter as they arrive in the winter season, will require them to go shopping for appropriate footwear, outerwear and hats and gloves immediately upon arrival.

A clothing list to provide to students can be found in the Appendix and it can be shared with the student prior to arrival so that they might be able to go shopping before they arrive to Canada. Should warm clothing stores not be available in the place of origin if a student is arriving from a tropical destination, the list will prove useful for the first shopping trip in Canada.

WEATHER

An international student needs to be made aware of the unstable weather in Canada and how a single day can have four season conditions.

Explain the importance of downloading a weather app on their cellphone and checking it every morning before leaving the residence in order to be appropriately prepared for changing weather conditions. Show the student how to layer clothing to adapt to changing conditions.

Some students are not aware of the dangers of frostbite and being unprepared for winter weather when waiting for public transportation or a school bus and this situation needs to be

clearly outlined to them. For example, many will not feel the cold initially and believe they do not need hats or mittens or gloves to protect their extremities. Others will wear shoes in winter ice conditions resulting in slips and falls and personal injury requiring hospital or clinic visits and absence from school. Similarly, not wearing other footwear appropriately can lead to injury.

This really happened!

A student decided to skate down the driveway of the home and onto the icy roadway after a winter ice storm left roads and sidewalks treacherous. The student did not know how to skate and had never worn skates before, not knowing that skating is an activity done on designated rinks only.

A student was not used to wearing boots and chose to wear them as slip on footwear rather than tie them up securely walking on icy sidewalks. He sprained his ankle as he slipped on the ice and the boots yielded no support. He had to be driven by the host to school every day and picked up at the end of the day for one week, adding responsibility and time to the host's day in addition to wait time at the walk-in clinic and lab for x-rays on the day of the incident. He wore ice cleats on his boot soles for the rest of the winter.

Trying skating for the first time, a student did not know how to tie up skates properly and attempted to exit the changeroom at an outdoor venue, only to have a number of adults jump to stop the student, ask him to sit down and in proper Canadian fashion, each grabbing one of his legs and tying up both skates for him. This intervention caught the student off guard and required a debrief explanation by the host as the student visibly got upset at this 'interference'.

TRANSPORTATION

Students in Canada will generally walk, cycle or ride a bus to get to school, either by yellow school bus or public transportation in large cities. More students are driven to school today by parents than ever before. It is important that the student know the way to school if he or she is not living on campus.

Public transportation orientation is important and websites, apps and bus stops locations should be explained, shown and visited, prior to the student's first day of school. A dry run of the bus route to take and stops to know is also a good practice exercise for students who have never used public transportation in their home countries. Some may not be familiar with subways, trams and light rapid rail systems

because they come from small cities or towns in their home country.

For example, students in Brazil are driven to school by parents, chauffeurs or private companies as public transportation is unsafe in large urban centres.

If a student is offered a ride to school one day, he or she may infer that they can ask for a ride every day and it sets a precedent and expectation on the host. In order to avoid this situation, inform the student that a ride will only be offered in extenuating circumstances unless it is offered as part of the homestay or school attendance agreement.

Students are generally responsible for their own transportation while in Canada. Some older students may know how to drive and have the funds to purchase their own vehicle and drive to school themselves. They need to know that an international driver's licence is required to drive in Canada, as the licence to drive from the country of origin will expire after 90 days. A Canadian licence, depending on the province of residence, will be required if they plan to stay longer and continue driving. Students should be made familiar with drinking and driving and cellphone use laws when driving and associated fines.

Adapting to Life in Canada

APPLIANCE USE: BATHROOM, LAUNDRY, KITCHEN

Depending on the facilities where students are accommodated when they arrive in Canada, they may share common spaces such as the bathroom, laundry room or kitchen or they may have their own. For instance, many older student residence buildings have a common bathroom on the same floor to be shared by multiple students, or they may be in a shared room setting with a bathroom for those two students only, or a shared bathroom in a home used by several household members.

BATHROOM

Some students arriving from different parts of the world may be used to having their own private bathroom and have never had to share a bathroom before. Bathrooms in different parts of the world also have different configurations. Students may be unfamiliar with using toilets, how to flush, shower function, bathtub use or electrical outlets for shaving and hair dryers.

Additional instructions are helpful to these students to integrate this new way of co-habitation. See the Appendix for a sample bathroom information sheet.

Written instructions posted in the bathroom, such as the ones found in hotel rooms to inform guests about towel use and ecological practices are useful means of informing a student on the customs of bathroom use. Disposal of feminine hygiene products also have to be specifically displayed, especially if a home is on a septic system as opposed to city water infrastructure.

LAUNDRY

Laundry practices and laundry spaces also vary greatly around the world. A student will need to be given specific instructions on the day, time and location for doing his or her laundry. Some students may not have ever done their own laundry before, coming from a household where domestic help does this task for the entire family. The student may not ask for instructions, or assume they know how to do the task, only to end up ruining their clothes or causing a malfunction with a washing machine by overloading it.

Some students will want to hang wet clothing in their bedroom for privacy reasons (such as washing undergarments or intimate apparel) or may bring wet towels from the bathroom into the bedroom and leave them on the floor, back of the chair or on top of a dresser causing water staining.

Provide students with specific instructions on how to wash their clothing, where to hang it if they don't want to use the dryer and how to hang it, so it will dry properly. If a student comes from a tropical zone, dryers may be unfamiliar appliances and they may be surprised to find out that clothes cannot be displayed or hung to dry outdoors, as some Canadian cities have municipal bylaws prohibiting outdoor clotheslines.

Electricity costs vary across the country and if there are different charges for varying hours of the day, your student should be made aware of the designated day and time to do laundry to limit hydro charges.

Students may need additional coaching, so do not assume they have understood the first time you show them how to use a machine. Supervision of them using the machine for the first three times they do laundry is always a good idea. Checking up on the machine after a few weeks once a laundry load has been started is also advisable.

Some families where a student might stay may not wish for the student to use the laundry machines and offer to do their laundry for them. This offer must come with an explanation for the student to understand this practice, so that he or she understands it is related to that family only and may not apply if the student moves to different accommodation.

KITCHEN

Students come with various levels of knowledge about kitchen use and food preparation. If coming from a family where food is always prepared for the student, he or she may not even know how to use a toaster, electric kettle or microwave oven.

It is always best to ask the student what they know about each appliance and how comfortable he or she is preparing food to eat. There may be a need to do a lot of coaching upon arrival and supervise the student in the kitchen before assuming that he or she can make something for himself or herself to eat.

Whether a student is allowed to do any cooking in a kitchen is a personal choice. If a student resides in residence, all meals will be provided but students may have access to a mini-kitchen on a residence floor to prepare a hot snack using a microwave oven, toaster and electric kettle for boiling water. These three appliances should be accessible to students in a home kitchen as well, to nurture some independence for the student.

Unfortunately, some host families and persons having international students who want to cook their own meals have had unpleasant experiences leading to the student being asked to leave a home. Some examples are students baking pizzas at 1 am and setting off the smoke detector, students cooking on the stove while the host was out, ruined pots and pans from high heat frying and cooking utensils and dishes left dirty in the sink.

If students are allowed to cook, they will also be buying their own food and expecting space in the refrigerator or freezer. Some families have been overrun with student food shopping and have been squeezed out of their own fridge and freezer space.

Once a student is allowed to do their own cooking, it is very difficult to reverse this path and may lead to increased friction

between the host and student, as the student begins to feel more entitlement towards the use of every space in the home. It is important to establish clear expectations and rules at the outset and revisit these rules with the student if the host does not want to provide meals to the student as part of their accommodation fee. The key to a successful placement is communication of expectations.

A full homestay arrangement includes room and board, which is three meals a day. Some students will skip breakfast, pack a lunch or buy their own food at a school cafeteria and come home to eat a supper meal. A sandwich lunch may be unfamiliar to international students where in most other parts of the world, lunch is considered a full hot meal and is often served as part of the school day either for free or for a lunch fee. They may find a sandwich unpalatable or insufficient for lunch. A compromise to this situation is to make an extra portion at supper/ dinner time and have enough to take as leftovers for lunch the next day in a plastic container.

Mealtime routines are also important to explain to a student. If the household eats at a particular time in the evening, the student should be made aware of this custom. Some families hold to a specific time and some households are busier and more flexible in time. Also be aware that dinner time varies across the world: students from hot countries eat later in the evening, between 7 and 9 pm, even as late as 10 pm and they may not be used to being hungry initially for supper at 5 pm or 6 pm. Allow some transition time for them.

Equally in some countries, breakfast or lunch is the meal eaten together with others and students might find the bagel, muffin, cereal and dashing to work or school very different from what they are used to. Similarly, they may be surprised at only having 30 to 40 minutes for lunch and find it difficult to rush through their meal. All of these customs will take some time to get used to, so explaining meal culture, within the resident household, school and work culture is very important. Students who have difficulty adjusting to these new ways, often fall sick or their physical or mental health is compromised in different ways, since food is an important source of comfort.

Teach them the recycling routines used in the local community which pertain to the residence where they are accommodated.

HEATING, WATER USE AND HYDRO

HEATING AND COOLING

International students from warm and tropical countries may find transitioning to cooler weather difficult, as they will be unfamiliar with the concept of heating a space to stay

warm. They will require coaching in layering their clothing to transition from indoors to outdoors. Some students will keep their winter coats on inside the home or school if they are cold, not understanding that the coat will not keep them warm once they return outdoors in the frigid cold.

Regulating body temperature to outdoor temperature is a concept that will be foreign to students who regularly only wear T-shirts and shorts and a light sweater when it is cooler.

Additionally, helping a student to purchase winter footwear, hats, mitts and thermal undergarments is very important because they do not know how the cold can affect their health and cause frostbite. See the suggested clothing list in the Appendix.

> This really happened!
>
> A student staying with a host family was too timid to indicate that the bedroom was too cold. The host observed the student wearing a winter coat at the desk through the bedroom window. It was discovered that the window had been unlatched and remained frozen open and it was winter but the student chose to compensate rather than inform the host of his discomfort.
>
> Another student arrived from a tropical country in January and was used to sleeping on the floor in his home country. Bedding was pulled off the bed and placed on the carpeted floor in the bedroom. Additionally, the student purchased a small portable heater and ran it continuously until the host noticed the door and door handle to the room was warm. The student had heated the room to 36 degrees Celsius to mimic his home country climate, nearly causing a fire in the host's home.

Students also need to know how temperature is regulated indoors, particularly if the heating is set to a lower temperature at night, requiring warm pajamas and additional blankets and duvets to stay warm. They need to be informed about the costs related to heating and why temperature extremes inside to outside are avoided to stay healthy.

If a student comes from a country where air conditioning is not used, they will open windows for fresh air, not realizing that this strains the air cooling system. Many students from warm countries find air conditioning too cold in homes, offices, public transportation and shopping malls. They need explanations that air conditioning is used to remove humidity causing excessive discomfort, which they may not experience in their home country.

WATER USE

Depending on the municipality regulations where the student is living, he or she must be made aware of cost of water usage in their accommodation. Some students can take multiple showers a day and will take showers up to 30 minutes if not restricted, or not turn off the tap correctly, leaving the water running for a prolonged period without being noticed. Ecological flush toilets with two settings also need to be explained. Day and time of doing laundry may also be tied to water consumption restrictions for environmental protection.

Alternatively, students coming from regions of the world where water is sparse or heavily restricted, need to be encouraged to shower daily and use water to improve personal hygiene

practices and do laundry weekly, as the generally accepted norm in our culture.

> **This really happened!**
>
> A student discovered the pleasure of taking a bath to enjoy bathing as there were only showering facilities in the home country. However, the ritual became a daily one and the host family needed to intervene as the hot water tank was emptied daily and water costs increased with this habit. The student also usurped the use of the main bathroom for two hours during this ritual every day after school.

HYDRO

Electricity consumption also varies around the world but students need to know how Canadians conserve energy in their own communities. Encourage students to turn off lights when not in use and provide a nightlight for the bathroom and bedroom if they are afraid of the darkness until they are familiar with their new living accommodations.

If a residence is heated by hydro, the concept of static electricity may be unfamiliar to a student. Explain the purpose of fabric softener sheets in the dryer and humidifiers to remove static electricity. Winter heat and dryness may also make skin dry. Take the time to show the student hand and body lotion and lip balm to reduce skin dryness in winter.

Some students may arrive with their own electrical adaptors, converters or transformers from their own country where voltage is 220V. Always ask the student to show electronics brought with them to determine if they can plug them in to the wall socket or require an adapter. Many adapters are made in China and are not compatible when plugged into wall outlets, even though they show voltage conversion. These have caused shorts and blown fuses in some family homes.

Always have one adapter available to the student and indicate where more adapters can be purchased locally. North America uses 110V for electrical outlets.

FAMILY STRUCTURES AND INCLUSION

International students arriving from many different countries will have some culturally specific notions of family and couples generated from their home country's political landscape, heritage, religion and family values. Explaining Canada's multicultural demographic, freedom of speech and association, freedom to practice the religion of one's choice and societal trends will be important information as students transition to life in Canada.

Laws related to same sex marriage, Lesbian Gay Bisexual Transgender Queer/Questioning and 2 spirited (LGBTQ2) terminology and perspectives are important for consideration in helping them learn about understanding Canadian inclusion and values placed on human rights, equity, and tolerance.

Common law relationships, various blended family structures (through separation, divorce and remarriage or living together) and single parent families may all be new concepts. The absence of intergenerational families or extended family members living close by or in the same home may be surprising to foreign students. Geographical distance, job opportunity and travel play a large part in family dispersion in Canada and this can explain why contact with family members can become limited.

First Nations Metis & Inuit (FNMI) populations and recognition of past wrongs suffered by those communities and efforts for reconciliation (such as recognition of traditional territory at the opening of conferences and events) are important elements of Canadian culture and evolving values.

Resources can be made available to students through their school's student services centre, through the local community agencies and trusted websites. Students need to know that hate literature, references, jokes and targeting of individuals can have serious consequences including criminal charges.

COMMUNICATION: VERBAL AND NON VERBAL COMMUNICATION (BODY LANGUAGE)

Having good communication with international students is very important in making them feel welcome, develop trust, become resourceful and know how to seek help if needed.

Check in frequently with students by reaching out to them to ask how they are feeling, if they are homesick, if they need help to find something or particular information. Taking initiative to communicate and probe the student will contribute to relationship building. If the student is very introverted, this initiative may provide security to them and assure them that an adult cares about their well-being far from their home country.

Asking about their family, pets, favourite colour, preferred subjects, sports, meals and drinks, and how their day went, are all examples of daily exchanges that will build communication and help with transitions for them.

Generally, students from warm or tropical regions tend to be more animated, conversant and interested in their experiences and open to telling about them, than students from more reserved or conservative cultures, colder regions or with less proficiency with the language. However, it will mostly depend on the character and personality of the student which may or may not coincide with a cultural stereotype described above.

VERBAL COMMUNICATION

When speaking with international students upon arrival keep exchanges brief and short and functional in nature, responses that can be answered with 'yes' and 'no', catering more to their personal needs and the routines they need to learn.

As time passes, opportunities for more dialogue in informal ways will occur and students may be more open about themselves and their past experiences, family life and study plans. Engaging with students in verbal interaction helps them build language skills and integrate local expressions. This process may take anywhere from a few days to several months depending on the comfort level of the student, their personality and language skills.

From the very beginning provide written back up to verbal instructions with sticky notes, text messages to the student's cellphone, written instructions, email and photos to illustrate an unfamiliar object, topic or place.

If a language other than English is spoken in a home, switching to English is considerate in the presence of the student.

NON-VERBAL COMMUNICATION

Body language is a form of communication that requires observation and intuition to perceive and integrate along with verbal messages or when nothing is spoken to illustrate an opinion, thought or reaction.

In many parts of the world it is more important than the spoken word.

It is also the most misinterpreted form of communication world wide and can lead to many mixed messages and misunderstandings or cultural 'faux-pas' (missteps) that people commit.

Although it presents as a very complex form of human behaviour, some essentials are important to note when interacting with newly arrived international students.

For example:

- Do not insist that the student look you in the eye when speaking with you (in some cultures looking down denotes respect to the speaker)
- Handshakes may be taboo when they are cross-gender (ie males shaking a female's hand would be considered very inappropriate or vice -versa)
- Nodding of the head or bowing the upper body is a greeting and sign of respect
- Placing hands together as if in prayer is acknowledgment of a message and sign of respect
- A student's non response may be a result of not understanding that they are being spoken to and expected to give a response, inadequate words to express a response, total or partial lack of comprehension, or confusion and fear if a student believes a response may compromise him or her in some way
- Frowning may be a sign of lack of comprehension or confusion (not annoyance or bad mood)
- Not speaking for several days may be a sign of depression not anger or resentment
- Rapid eye blinking may be a sign of distress
- Many cultures use hand gestures to amplify the verbal message and it is not a sign of over excitability or hyperactivity
- Loud volume does not always denote anger
- Looking up, to the side or away may be a sign of embarrassment or also verbal overload requiring more processing time

EXTRACURRICULAR ACTIVITIES AND SPORTS, FITNESS

Students may or may not engage in extracurricular sports or clubs at school as this may not have been offered to them in the home country where school had strictly an academic purpose. It may take some time for them to realize that these additional school offerings form an integrated part of an education for high school and post-secondary students in Canada.

Some may inquire to join a local gym or a familiar sport activity to them (badminton, tennis, soccer) and this is an important element of integrating into a new culture and making new friends. Help provide them with information on where these facilities and programs are located and offered.

At times, their preferred sport may not be widely known or practiced in Canada (such as rugby or cricket) and this may present an opportunity to try a Canadian sport such as skating, hockey, snow shoeing or skiing/snowboarding in winter or kayaking, swimming or cycling in summer.

Be aware that some students may not know how to swim, ride a bike or drive a car, which are activities that young people would normally learn in Canada.

It is advisable to highlight the importance of staying healthy in winter and summer for students, even if this means just going for a walk outside, discovering a nature trail or hiking and enjoying the outdoors. Students who are from dense urban cities may not have had an opportunity to experience nature close at hand and may be afraid of doing so in fear of animals (even dogs, such as they will see the propensity of Canadians who own and walk their dogs) like wolves, bears and other animals they may have heard about that are present in Canada and which they may believe roam everywhere, including in cities.

CUSTOMS: A BIT OF 'CANADIANA' AND TRANSITIONING TO LIVING LIKE A LOCAL

It is always great when a student engages in learning everything about their new country of residence and the study abroad opportunity. Some students may be living a dream they have cultivated since being a young child, and may have researched much about Canada prior to arrival.

Others may have been sent here to study to fulfill a family's goal or expectation and they have very high demands placed on them for being successful. They may believe that studying continuously is essential because they are in constant communication with family members back home who are reinforcing these expectations for them in a regular way.

This messaging often comes into conflict once they interact and integrate with local students who may not have such demanding expectations placed on them and who value some fun and friendship, and experience more of what Canadian youth enjoy during school and study periods.

Try to include them with your family traditions and ask them about their own so that he/she can become even more part of your family. They might find a new hobby that they never had before.

Show students places to visit to become familiar with things to see and experience in the local neighbourhood, larger community, nearby urban centre, shows and events and sporting venues.

On holidays, explain how families travel to see each other, visit other places, eat certain foods and have a good time away from home and the routine of school and work.

Explain the meaning of Canadian symbols:

Allow them to experience Canadian products:

Exposure to local favourites specific to regions in Canada can also complement food and drink experiences.

If they are over legal drinking age in the province or territory they reside in, a taste of local wine, craft beer and liquors native to the area also enhance their appreciation for this country.

TRANSITIONING TIME FOR STUDENTS

How long it takes a student to transition to their new country depends on many factors: previous travel experience from the home country, comfort level in the new language, prior visits to the new country, other family members or friends who are in the new country, personality, interests, goals and expectations of the family or individual and the welcome they receive through their first impressions and interactions in Canada.

Students will transition in their own way and according to their own rhythm and interests. They will naturally gravitate to other international students from their own culture first and form friendships with those individuals as an initial support network. This initiative should be encouraged as part of the landing phase in the transition period.

Imposing upon students that they speak only in English or French will have an adverse effect and interfere with the natural progression of second or additional language learning. Students should be housed initially with another student from their home country in a dormitory or residence situation. There needs to be a linguistically safe space for them to relax, reflect, share experiences and have downtime to recover. Functioning in an unfamiliar language for several hours a day will be cognitively exhausting and stressful for them and they will often express that they feel tired.

As part of this cognitive effort, students will also experience more hunger and want to sleep a lot as part of their transition period, especially in the winter months. These elements are natural and should be satisfied in order to allow personal growth. Food is an important source of comfort and eating food from their own country during the transition also provides emotional nourishment. Access to culturally specific grocery or food stores should be made available to students during the transition period so that they may shop for some familiar food items.

Many students will continue to interact with family members and friends back home through video conferencing apps and platforms. This contact can help reduce homesickness as well, since it eliminates the effect of geographical distance from the home country. Nevertheless, ensure that they don't do this all the time as it will also worsen their homesickness.

A host can help with the transition by integrating the student in family events and treating them as his or her own children. A hosting agency should organize periodic trips, events and small excursions so that students make friends and learn about their surroundings.

It may take up to two years for students to acclimatize to their life in a new country and city and up to seven years to become academically proficient in English or French to the level of native speakers in Canada. Supporting students by offering help and encouraging them to ask questions to meet their needs will go a long way to making them feel welcome and comfortable in their new home. Offering to take them shopping initially and later on short excursions and day trips to local points of interest will help them learn about their community, town or city.

Health and Personal Safety

PHYSICAL HEALTH

Many students will bring a variety of over the counter supplements and products with them in case they fall ill. If they take any medications, they must inform you, as it is critical to know if there are any health or medical conditions which may require emergency interventions such as asthma, heart conditions, diabetes or other health situations.

Students should be made aware of seasonal conditions which may exist for residents in various parts of Canada such as allergies. Informing them about common Canadian practices regarding flu shots, vitamin supplements and immunizations offered through school- based clinics is also important.

Locate the nearest pharmacy and walk-in medical clinic so that students know where to go in case they are not feeling well. Explain that hospitals are only for emergency life threatening situations or acute care symptoms (breathing, bleeding, broken bones). They need to know that they will be required to pay upfront for medical services, whether in a clinic, lab or hospital and let them know what these costs are in your local area by calling these establishments.

> **This really happened!**
>
> A student requested the host to take him to the hospital because of swelling from a bug bite on the arm. The host indicated that the appropriate intervention was to go to a walk-in clinic if topical creams did not help. The student indicated that clinic doctors were not as good as hospital doctors, a belief brought from the home country. The student required a briefing on how clinics and hospitals differed in purpose and how all doctors have certification regardless of where they practice.
>
> A host family only found out that the student staying with them had a heart condition when a scary situation occurred with the student. Neither the student nor the agency which placed the student had informed the host that the student had a heart condition for which medication was being taken. Disclosure of health information is often held back by international student applicants and their families for fear of being denied a study permit or visa, or by placement agencies to avoid refusal by a family for the placement of the student. Hosts do have a right to know important health information for the student residing with them in order to properly care for their needs.
>
> Another student requested a visit to the hospital for a facial blemish. She insisted that it was an infection and not a pimple, which she was unaccustomed to having. Discussion was needed to point out that the newly acquired acne could be due to a diet change. The student was eating cookies regularly in her room and drinking 2 to 3 cans of carbonated drinks a day, behaviours that were not allowed at home. Acne medication was introduced and a suggestion towards better eating habits.

Encourage students to eat well, get enough sleep, exercise and avoid late nights, especially in the winter months. Gym memberships and sports leagues are excellent for physical fitness and socializing purposes either through school or in the community. Students who are passionate about a sport will often seek out these opportunities.

MENTAL HEALTH

Sometimes students are sent to study in Canada with only a one- way ticket which can be a traumatic experience for the young person if they have never left home before. Feelings of abandonment coupled with high expectations to perform in an unfamiliar country and education system can be overwhelming.

Many students spend school vacation periods in Canada either because it is too expensive to return to the home country for a one, or a two week period, or their parents have not allowed them to return until the summer break, or not at all.

This situation can be heartbreaking but happens regularly, particularly for many students from Asia. Without a peer support network and a key adult to assist them, students become very vulnerable to mental health distress and breakdown. Provide students with mental health support services in their own language which can be accessed through online resources in various languages in every province.

This really happened!

A student had been relocated several times to various host families within a short period of arrival. It was observed that personal hygiene was problematic, the bedroom was in chronic disorder, frequent loud angry interactions occurred through video conferencing which became uneasy for the host family to hear, and cooked food refuse was found in the dresser drawers of the bedroom where the student stayed. He also made no progress at school over several months and appeared constantly distressed. The student had difficulty communicating and was clearly unhappy. He was forced to stay over the summer for summer school as he had not achieved expected results from a parental perspective. When the student left the host family, the room required repainting due to the walls being used by the student to wipe fingers and the carpet removed due to accumulated food and drink stains, despite not being allowed to eat in the room which the student continued to do, part of his inability to follow rules and routines.

Watching for signs of failing mental health in a student is also critical, as timely intervention can assist in identifying the source of the problem. Symptoms of mental health distress may appear in a variety of ways and is as individual as the student. Some common flags to look for are:

- the student is isolating himself or herself in his or her room and won't socialize, even basic exchanges with others in the residence
- talks of home constantly and appears homesick
- late to school on a daily basis
- looks overly tired, sleeps a lot
- eats little or excessively
- does not speak of having any friends, does not speak
- does not go out for fun
- studies continuously with no break
- is heard arguing over video calls
- looks unhappy, never laughs or smiles
- room is unkept, messy and full of garbage
- personal hygiene is neglected
- routines and expectations are not followed
- evidence of substance use or abuse

Encourage them to seek help and advice from school social workers, cultural key contact persons at school or on campus or student services centres.

It is important to notify the student's agent or homestay coordinator and have their contact information on hand in case the student spirals downwards, abandons studies, disappears or otherwise cannot be reached or located. The study visa or permit is contingent on the student regularly attending school and can be revoked if the student no longer attends classes.

Immigration services can become involved when deportation is possible, if the student becomes involved in illicit activity, commits an offence or is accused of a crime.

PERSONAL SAFETY

Students should always feel safe in their accommodation, preferably with a door that can be locked from the inside for privacy. They should be provided with their own house key for entry or their own combination for automatic key lock entry systems.

They need to know 911 information, how to call and what to report.

They also need to know not to carry a large amount of cash (for example over $100) as Canada is a debit and credit economy for the most part. Cash may be more frequently used in smaller communities.

> This really happened!
>
> Even after being explained the fire escape drill, and briefed on a safety evacuation drill, a student did not come out of the bedroom when the smoke detector went off. The student continued to work on homework and listen to music indicating that they heard the alarm but did not know what it meant. The demonstration exercise had failed to sound the alarm so that the student could recognize the sound of the alarm and take action as per the drill instructions.
>
> Many countries do not have smoke detectors and the fire hazard to buildings in Canada are also unfamiliar to international students as they do not associate the correct level of danger to such an alarm.

Travelling at night in large urban centres and using mass transportation systems, taxis and Ubers are also part of personal safety planning. Cycling and driving information is essential if students begin to commute this way. Fire escape information, carbon monoxide and smoke detector sounds should be explained to them and demonstrated, as many students will be unfamiliar with these devices and their purpose.

THE GUIDE TO HOSTING INTERNATIONAL STUDENTS IN CANADA

This really happened!

A group of international students were involved in what appeared to be a confrontation as perceived by passersby. The police were summoned and students charged for uttering threats and physical assault. Students may not be aware that they can face criminal charges for behaviour that is deemed culturally acceptable in their own culture at home (verbal exchanges, pushing or shoving with bodily contact, gestures, loud exchanges).

Some international students have faced dangerous driving offences or criminal charges because of deaths caused by motor vehicle accidents in which the driver was an international student. Apart from the tragedy of having studies cut short and facing judicial processes, if victims are killed as pedestrians or vehicle occupants, there is additional trauma to the international student.

It is similarly traumatic to a foreign family to be informed of the loss of, or injury to, their child overseas in an unfamiliar country, regardless of age.

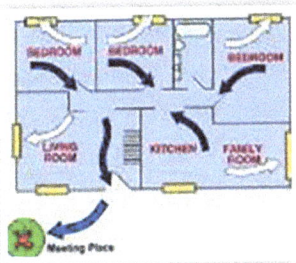

Additionally, aggressive physical contact can be construed as assault by bystanders, loud verbal exchanges between two people can be interpreted as harassment and a safety issue, placing a person in danger. Citizens can video these events using their cellphones and provide footage to police in order to lay charges.

International students must be made aware of proper decorum in public spaces, including school common areas, public transportation and open spaces or in shopping malls. Any disturbance will cause security services to investigate and international students may find themselves in a compromising situation if they are not aware of what is socially acceptable behaviour in public.

However, students also need to know their rights and how to complain to a person in authority at school or in public, and telling a trusted adult if they fall victim of a crime, are mislead and trapped in a situation of extortion or exploitation, or hurt and threatened in any manner. They may feel as though they are to blame, feel shame, insecure or think it will bring disrepute to their families if they speak up about what troubles them. This stance often causes them more danger and harm if it remains unaddressed.

> This really happened!
>
> Chinese students were contacted and told that harm would come to their families in China if they did not pay a ransom before a deadline. Often international students come from wealthy families with padded bank accounts in Canada and at home and there are many scams to prey on their vulnerability. All threats need to be reported promptly to authorities.

Conclusion

This guide was designed to provide basic information to individuals involved in welcoming and hosting international students who may have no prior experience in doing so. Many different components combine to make an international student successful in his or her new learning and living environment and many items presented in this guide should be adapted to the local community in which the host or hosting institution is located.

International students can enrich the community in many ways, just as Canadians can enrich the lives of students through the many qualities known throughout the world as qualifying a Canadian: polite, kind, helpful and resourceful.

A maturing Canada depends on newcomers for its continued economic prosperity, cultural diversity and stories of success. The international student demographic plays into all three of these areas and promotes the best our nation has to offer.

APPENDIX 1

SAMPLE INSTRUCTIONS FOR STUDENTS

HOW TO USE A WAFFLE MAKER

1. Plug in waffle maker to outlet on wall.
2. Wait for green light
3. Lift cover. Turn on stove fan to take smoke away.
4. Spray top and bottom panels with cooking oil spray
5. Spoon a ladle full of batter onto the bottom grid panel
6. Clover cover – wait 10 seconds
7. Flip handle clockwise
8. Wait for green light and turn back counter clockwise
9. Open lid and remove waffle
10. Pull out cord from wall socket to unplug the appliance.

TO MAKE PANCAKES

1. Turn on stove to maximum heat and fan
2. Pour a small amount of oil into the frying pan
3. Wait until oil slides easily around the pan
4. Turn down heat to medium
5. Pour one spoonful of batter into frying pan for each pancake (maximum 4 per cooking time)
6. Wait until pancake surface begins to bubble
7. Flip pancake and wait 1-2 minutes
8. Turn off stove
9. Remove pancakes onto plate
10. Place frying pan on another burner on the stove to cool.

APPENDIX 2

POSTING RULES AND EXPECTATIONS

WELCOME TO MY HOME! IN THE BEDROOM....

1. Please keep door closed.
2. No eating or food in the bedroom. Please eat in the kitchen.
3. No drinks in room except for water bottle or glass of water.
4. Quiet time is from 10 pm. Lights off at 11 pm.
5. Listen to music or talk on the phone with headphones or earbuds.
6. Take a shower once a day before 10 pm.
7. Place paper, cans, glass and plastic in blue recycling box and all other trash in the garbage can.
8. Always keep your room neat and tidy for room check.
9. Use laundry basket for dirty clothes. Your laundry time is _____
10. Clean and vacuum your room once a week on _____

<u>House rules:</u>

11. Always have your house key with you when you leave.
12. **Always lock the front door when you enter or leave the house.**
13. Text a message by 5 pm if you will not be home for supper.

Homestay rules:

14. Be home by 9 pm every night. On Friday and Saturday nights, be home by 11 pm.
15. Text your plans to the host and tell him or her when you go out.

WHEN SHARING THE BATHROOM WITH OTHERS:

1. **Toilet**: Use HALF flush for pee (urine) and FULL flush for poo (feces). Wipe down toilet seat if soiled.
2. **Shower:** Shower time is 10 minutes maximum. Close shower curtain before showering and keep it inside the bathtub. Shower head must point forward to keep water inside the tub. Keep folded hand towel on bathtub ledge to absorb water. Hang floor towel over side of bathtub after shower and close shower curtain to dry when you are finished showering. Keep slip mat in tub.
3. **Please shower before 10 pm.**
4. **Fan:** Turn on the fan when you take a shower, or when you sit on the toilet (to take the odour out of the bathroom).
5. **Sink and counter**: Wipe up water around the sink and on the counter with the hand towel to keep it clean for the next person.
6. **Towels:** keep all towels in the bathroom. Hang towels on towel rack or on hook on back of door to dry.
7. **Door:** Always leave the door wide open when no one is in the bathroom (for air circulation).
8. **Empty plastic containers** go in the blue recycling box in your bedroom. Used tissues and products go in the garbage can.

BATHROOM CULTURAL CUE CARD FOR PERSONAL HYGIENE BELOW:

FOR FEMININE HYGIENE PRODUCTS

PADS

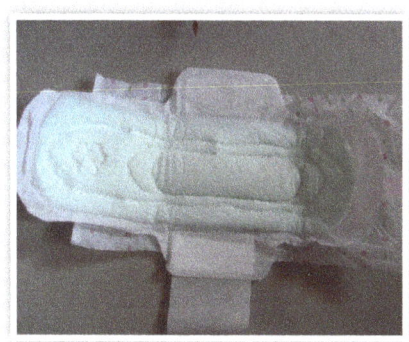 

ROLL USED PADS INTO TOILET PAPER AND PLACE IN GARBAGE CAN

TAMPONS

FLUSH IN TOILET USING FULL FLUSH

USING A DOUBLE FLUSH ECO-TOILET

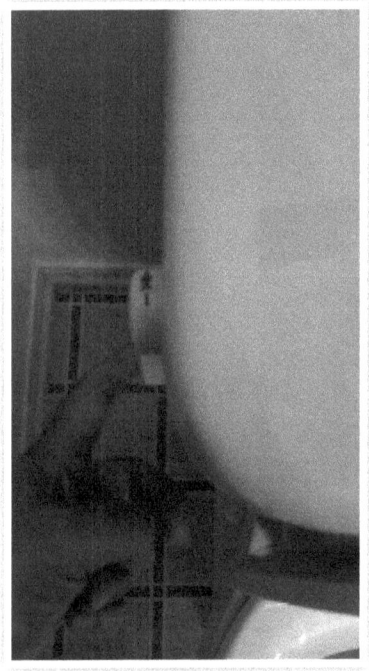

**PULL FORWARD
FOR HALF-FLUSH**

(LESS WATER)

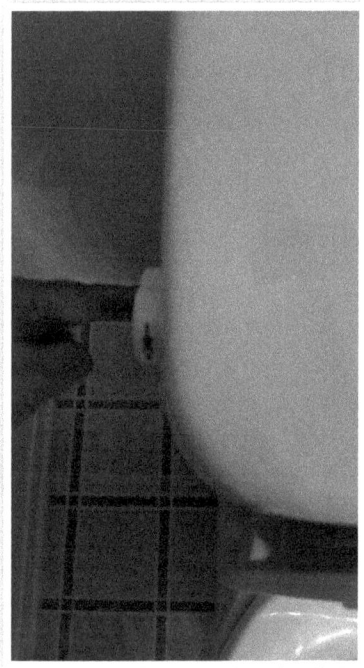

**PUSH BACK FOR
FULL FLUSH**

(MORE WATER)

IN THE KITCHEN....

1. Use plain dishes to heat in the microwave. **Please use the plastic cover over your plate when you heat food.**
2. Unplug toaster oven, toaster and hot water kettle after using it.
3. Flower dishes are only for serving meals on the table.
4. After eating, separate items for recycling:
   a) All food scraps go in the metal bucket under the sink.
   b) All glass, foam or plastic containers in sink for rinsing.
   c) All wrapping in the garbage can.
   d) Leave paper wrapping and egg cartons on the counter.
5. **Place dirty dishes and glasses in the sink and fill them with water.**
6. Wipe table after eating with sink cloth.
7. After supper, heat food in microwave only or have a cold snack.
8. Check dishwasher for clean forks, knives and spoons and dishes if you can't find something.
9. Refill the BRITA water filter container in the fridge if you finish the last amount and leave it on the counter.
10. If you eat the last of food or there is no more left (eggs, milk, bread) or if you need a special item, please write it on the white paper sheet on the shelf above the counter.

Thank you!

CLOTHING LIST FOR WINTER

- Hat or tuque that covers the ears (2)
- Mitts and gloves for fall and winter (2-4)
- Fleece or wool sweaters, sweatshirts (2-3)
- Long sleeved T-shirts, cotton turtleneck shirts or thermal undershirts (4-5)
- Warm socks that rise above the ankle
- Winter boots
- Scarf or shawl, facemask (balaclava)
- Substantial winter coat with a hood
- Ice cleats for boot soles in snowy communities

Contact the author for sample private homestay agreements to use with minor students and adult students.
www.horizoned.ca

ABOUT THE AUTHOR

Monika Ferenczy is an Education Consultant who helps students and parents make decisions regarding learning and education. Her practice focuses on finding the best solution to meet the needs of students, young or mature, to help them reach their full potential. Providing relevant and timely information is critical for sound decision-making and she assists all Canadian and international clients with the highest quality of service. Considered an expert in the education sector, Monika supports families with special needs children, offers education expertise in separation and divorce proceedings, presents workshops for young parents and advocates for improved educational practices, policies and legislation to government.

www.ingramcontent.com/pod-product-compliance
Lightning Source LLC
LaVergne TN
LVHW051226070526
838200LV00057B/4623